Personality Te _
(How Organizations are
Probing the Inner You)

Author: Paul E. Love

Copyright 2017 Paul E. Love

Other Books by the Author:

The Employer's Payroll Question and Answer Book
2017
Rescue Me: Animals in Need
The UAV Question and Answer Book
The Sports Dictionary
Find an IT Job

CONTENTS

Introduction..3

What is "Personality"?........................5

The History of Personality Theories & Testing...11

Personality Testing Examined..........15

The Case Against Personality Tests for Job Seekers...................................25

"Passing" a Personality Test............30

Experimenting with Personality Tests 33

Popular Tests – the 16 Personality Factor Test.....................................38

Popular Tests – the DISC Assessment 41

Popular Tests – the Caliper Profile...43

Sample Personality Assessments....44

Personality Tests for Kids...............46

Future Trends in Personality Testing 47

Appendix A – Terminology...............50

Introduction

Personality tests provide nothing more than a general guideline in analyzing a potential employee. Be aware that there's no hard evidence that personality tests are accurate measures of an individual's personality. People are a combination of character traits – some stronger, some weaker – and which traits show up the strongest can vary with the situation. Trying to categorize a person according to a given set of personality indicators may or may not give a true picture of the individual. Plus you might get considerably different results giving a prospect the same test a second time.

Dependence on personality tests can be so misleading that some firms that develop tests (such as Myers-Briggs) advise that using the their test for hiring purposes may even be unethical. People of varying personalities may all do well at a given job for different reasons. Personality may not accurately reflect or correspond to the ability to successfully fill a specific job opening. For example the late Steve Jobs exhibited a tendency toward introversion, not the best characteristic for a salesperson. But he was extremely successful presenting his ideas to the public.

Even the term "personality test" is misleading. A better term is "personality assessment", since "test" implies that there are right or wrong answers. When you're dealing with people's personalities there aren't right or wrong answers, just tendencies of one type or another. However, when a personality assessment is used to evaluate job applicants there may well be certain answers that give you a better chance at being hired. When you're being tested for a specific position your potential employer may be looking for people whose profile tends to fit those particular job requirements and the company culture.

So should you be worried about the prospect of taking a personality assessment as part of applying for a job? Worried may be too strong a term, but it could be to your advantage to know a little bit about personality testing ahead of time.

What is "Personality"?

Q: Where does the word "personality" come from?
A: The word "personality" stems from the Latin word *persona,* which refers to the masks worn by actors at one time to indicate the type of character they were portraying or to disguise their true identity.

Q: What is the definition of "personality"?
A: One definition is that an individual's personality is made up of the characteristic patterns of thoughts, feelings and behaviors that are unique to that person.

Q: Does my personality stay the same over the years?
A: Certain things – injuries, drugs, traumatic experiences – can influence your personality, but to a large extent your basic personality appears to remain fairly constant as you grow older.

Q: What determines the makeup of my personality?
A: There are different theories as to what influences the development of your

personality including:

- Trait theories which attribute people's personalities to genetic (inherited) characteristics.
- Type theories that are based on the idea that people's personalities fall into a number of distinct "personality types" that can be broken down into a basic set of characteristics which are related to biological influences.
- Behavioral theories which attribute personality development to the interaction between individuals and their environment.
- Psychodynamic theories that are closely related to the ideas of Sigmund Freud and emphasize the influence of the subconcious on personality development.

Q: What exactly is the trait theory of personality?
A: Trait theory focuses on the differences between individuals – comparative terms such as outgoing or introverted, kind or stern, calm or nervous. Personality, according to trait theory, is a result of the interaction of these different characteristics and an individual's personality can be determined by measuring the type and strength of the

these various traits.

There have been a number of attempts to identify the primary "traits" that determine an individual's personality:

- In 1936, Gordon Allport summarized over 4,000 words that indicated personality traits into three major groups:
  - Cardinal traits that dominate a person's whole life
  - Central traits that aren't as dominate, but generally define someone's personality – kind, intelligent, anxious, etc.
  - Secondary traits that relate to preferences or attitudes and only show up in specific circumstances (such as impatience when having to wait in line).
- Raymond Cattell reduced the list of traits down to 16 primary traits which he considered the building blocks of everyone's personality. Cattell also developed one of the most widely known personality tests, the Sixteen Personality Factor Questionnaire.
- Hans Eysenck developed a personality model based on just three key traits –

introversion/extraversion, neuroticism/emotional stability.

- A new theory – the "Big 5" theory – was eventually developed by researchers who felt that Cattell dealt with too many key factors and Eysenck dealt with too few factors. The Big 5 theory is based on five primary traits: extraversion, agreeableness, conscientiousness, neuroticism, and openness (openness to alternatives as opposed to conformity).

The major criticism of trait theory is that a individual's personality traits aren't a reliable indicator of how he or she will react in a given situation.

Q: What are personality disorders?
A: Personality disorders are classified as a type of mental illness. They involve thought patterns and behaviors that are unhealthy and potentially dangerous. While the cause of personality disorders is unknown they are generally thought to stem primarily from genetics and childhood experiences and usually begin during teenage years or early adulthood. Types of personality disorders include:

- Antisocial personality disorder –

Marked by a disregard of others' feelings or needs, aggressive or violent behavior, disregard for the safety of yourself and others, and a lack of remorse for harmful acts.

- Narcissistic personality disorder – Characterized by a belief that you're superior to and more important than others, arrogance, exaggeration of your abilities and talents, and a failure to recognize others' needs or feelings.
- Borderline personality disorder – Involves impulsive and risky behavior, a fragile self-image, intense but unstable relationships, fear of being left alone, intense mood swings, and, in many cases, suicidal behavior or threats of self-injury.
- Obsessive-compulsive personality disorder – Marked by a preoccupation with orderliness and rules, a need to be in control of other people and in charge of every situation, an inflexibility concerning ethics or morality, and an excessive commitment to work or projects. Note: This is not the same as obsessive-compulsive disorder, which is anxiety-related.
- Paranoid personality disorder –

Usually involves distrust and suspicion of others and their motives and an unjustified belief that other people are conspiring against you. It also tends to include an angry or hostile reaction to perceived slights or insults and a tendency to hold grudges.

- Schizoid personality disorder – Involves a lack of interest in forming any relationships, preferring to remain by yourself. It is also marked by an appearance of being cold and indifferent to others and an inability to enjoy or take part in normal activities.

The History of Personality Theories & Testing

Q: When did personality testing get its start?
A: Personality tests have been around in some form since at least 2000 B.C. Chinese emporers in the third century used them to judge intellect, knowledge and integrity when selecting civil servants.

Q: What was the first widespread theory of personality testing?
A: Hippocrates (and later Galen) postulated that a person's behavior was based on four different temperatments or body fluids, which Galen labeled blood, mucus, black bile and yellow bile. The dominant one of these four fluids was said to be a person's "humor". This theory was popular all through the Middle Ages.

Q: How long did the four fluids theory last and what replaced it?
A: Progress in medicine during the nineteenth century made it obvious that personality didn't have any direct connection with a person's bodily "fluids". In the late 19th century a physiologist

named Wilhelm Wundt postulated that four temperaments - sanguine, phlegm, cholera and melancholy – were the basis of human personality and that each person was a combination of two or more of these temperaments.

Q: What other types of personality testing were popular in the 18th and 19th centuries?
A: Two of the main methods of personality testing were Phrenology (personality assessment based on various measurements of the human skull) and Physiognomy (which theorized that personality was linked to outward appearance). Note: Interestingly, some recent studies indicate that good-looking individuals are often perceived as being more likeable and trustworthy.

Q: When did the study of human personality start to become widespread?
A: In the early 20th century researchers like Sigmund Freud, Carl Jung (a student of Freud's), and Eduard Spranger all developed theories about human behavior. Freud believed that there were three components of the human mind (the id, the ego and the superego) and that they struggled for dominance, and

the constant struggle between them was responsible for an individual's personality. Jung's theory was that people have four main ways of interacting with the world – intuition, thinking, feeling and sensing – and that we all use of those four methods as our preferred way of dealing with life.

Q: What is the Rorschach test?

A: The Rorschach inkblot test came into use in 1921 as a way to determine personality through the interpretation of abstract inkblots.

Q: What was John B. Watson's theory of personality?

A: Watson, who had a good deal of influence on others studying personality development, theorized that all actions performed by human beings, such as thinking, feeling and acting, should be considered behaviors. As a result of this idea that everything we think, feel or do represents a behavior, Watson and others who like him were labeled "behaviorists". According to them, genetics are unimportant – it's environment that shapes a person's intelligence, temperament and other personality traits.

Q: Who was Abraham Maslow?
A: Maslow was a well-known and respected American psychologist who developed a pyramid structure called the Hierarchy of Needs to help explain human personality development. His theory was that humans have certain needs that must be met, and that if the lower level psysiological and safety needs aren't being met then the person can't progress to higher levels such as self-esteem, morality and creativity.

Q: When was the first major use of personality testing in the United States?
A: The Woodworth Personal Data Sheet test was used during World War I for the psychiatric screening of new draftees.

Q: What was the first "modern era" personality test?
A: The Myers-Briggs test (developed by Katherine Briggs and her daughter Isabel Briggs Myers) involves questions based on Jung's theories. Myers-Briggs testing isn't designed to produce a "pass/fail" type of result – its purpose is simply to help the test-taker learn more about him or herself.

Personality Testing Examined

Q: Is personality testing a big business?

A: Personality testing is definitely a big business, with revenues currently estimated at 2 to 4 billion dollars a year and growing.

Q: What are some of the different types of personality tests currently in use?

A: The three main categories of personality assessments are:

- **Objective or self-report inventory tests** which consist of statements that the test-taker has to rate according to how much they agree or disagree with the statement (by choosing between responses such as "strongly agree", "slightly agree", "no opinion", "slightly disagree", or "strongly disagree"). In objective testing a certain pattern of answers means one thing, a different pattern indicates something else about the test-takers personality. The most commonly used objective test of personality is the Minnesota Multiphasic Personality Inventory

(MMPI).

- **Subjective tests** are similar to objective tests, except that there are no set patterns indicating certain personality traits – the test-taker's responses are open to interpretation.
- **Projective tests** in which test-takers respond to a series of items such as inkblots, pictures or incomplete sentences. The theory is that the test-takers will project their own feelings and attitudes in their answers.

Q: What are some of the most widely used tests used to explore and evaluate people's personalities?
A: Some of the more popular methods of personality testing are:

- **Myers Briggs Type Indicator Test** – Myers Briggs has been the most widely used personality test in recent years. It's designed around the theories of C. G. Jung and divides people into 16 distinct personality types, based on 8 identifiable traits: extroversion or introversion, sensing or intuition, thinking or feeling, and judging or perceiving. Note: The test's creators have warned that it should not be used for testing job applicants, since it isn't designed for that purpose.

- **Minnesota Multiphasic Personality Inventory** – MMPI tests consist of a set of true/false questions designed to assess 10 underlying personality traits such as hypochondria, masculinity/femininity, paranoia, and introversion or extroversion. Although it is used primarily to diagnose personality disorders, it has also found wide-spread use for non-clinical uses such as job applicant evaluation.
- **The Caliper Profile** – This test has been around for about 50 years and is often used to measure personality traits such as thoroughness, assertiveness, empathy and leadership ability that relate to qualities needed on the job.
  - Sample question: Job applicants are asked to select the one statement out of a group of statements that best reflects their own viewpoint and fill in the "most" circle on an answer sheet. From the remaining choices, they then select the

one statement that least reflects
their viewpoint, filling in the
"least" circle. For example:
- A. Sometimes it's better to
  lose than to risk hurting
  someone.
- B. I'm generally good at
  making "small talk."
- C. Established practices
  and/or standards should
  always be followed.
- D. I sometimes lose control
  of my workday.

- **Sixteen Personality Factor
  Questionnaire (or "16PF") -**
  Devised in 1949 by psychologist
  Raymond Cattell, the 16PF test is
  based on 16 personality traits that
  Cattell believed we all possess.
  There are 170 questions on the
  test and instead of trying to get
  you to describe your personality in
  some way, the 16PF asks you how
  you might react to different
  situations on the job. Test takers
  have to answer each question as
  "true", "false", or "I'm not sure". A
  sample question might be "When a
  bit of tact or convincing is needed
  to get people moving, I'm usually
  the one who does it".
- **Work Personality Index (WPI) -**

Designed by Dr. Donald MacNab and Shawn Bakker, the questionnaire is designed to identify personality traits that relate to work performance and usually takes between 15 to 20 minutes to complete. The WPI involves 17 primary scales that measure aspects of a person's at-work personality in order to make connections between the person's preferences and their work behavior. These 17 scales are categorized into five groups that provide an overview of your at-work personality: Achievement Orientation, Conscientiousness, Social Orientation, Practical Intelligence and Adjustment.

Q: What is "4-Quadrant" personality testing?
A: 4-Q assessments classify people into a combination of four different options, labeled with letters and numbers (or colors, animals, etc.). This type of assessment originated with a man named Empedocles around 450 B.C. 4-Q tests generally consist of a series of adjectives. The person taking the test chooses the words from the list that most describe him or her. Due to the

ability of test-takers to recognize desired answers and manipulate their responses accordingly, 4-Q tests have little value in evaluating job applicants.

Q: What are Situational Judgement tests?
A: Situational Judgement Tests (or "SJTs") consist of problems for the test-taker to resolve, but the problems don't have correct or incorrect answers. The test makers provide a scoring method that involves determining which answers are the most or least desirable. SJTs are usually untimed and focus more on practical know-how, rather than reasoning ability – plus they tend to be oriented toward a particular type of job.

Q: What factors go into a "good" personality test?
A: Factors to look for in a personality test include:
  - Tests that don't try to plug people into distinct categories, such as "prefers to work alone" versus "prefers to work with others". None of us fit into a particular category all the time.
  - The test should have multiple methods for determining an applicant's reliability.

Questions should be behavior-based. For example, "I'm comfortable bringing my suggestions to my superiors", rather than "I'm a confident person".

- It should measure the more stable traits that won't change significantly over time.
- You should be able to measure the test results of different applicants against each other in some meaningful way.
- Look for providers who are open about how they check the validity of their test, how they assess the accuracy of the test results.

Q: What are some additions or alternatives to the use of personality tests to evaluate job applicants?
A: References, quizzes, and simulated situations and exercises that actually test an applicant's knowledge, job skills and ability to apply his or her knowledge and skills. Employers who don't want to create their own assessment quizzes can find assessment tests for everything from Time Management to Telephone Etiquette at websites such as Brainbench or Expertrating.

Q: How successful are personality assessments in finding good employees?

A: The Aberdeen Group (www.aberdeen.com) has conducted a study of the use of personality testing and found a strong correlation between successful companies and the use of personality assessments to identify prospective employees. In fact, according to the Aberdeen study Best-in-Class companies were 69% more likely to use personality testing as part of the hiring process. The question however, is whether the personality assessments are responsible for the hiring of high quality employees or if other factors (such as astute hiring managers, additional testing or the attraction of job applicants to successful companies) play a major part in acquiring top talent.

Q: What are some examples of personality test questions and what the answers indicate?

A: Here are a few standard types of questions and what they indicate about the test-taker's personality traits:

- **I like parties and social events (true or false)** – A "true" answer may mean that you're sociable but not particularly independent – or even that you tend to be more of a follower than a leader.

- **I feel a little uneasy when people compliment me (strongly agree, agree, disagree, strongly disagree) –** This type of question is aimed at determining whether the test-taker is more of a strong, confident personality or tends to be humble and self-effacing.
- **I am better at most things than any of my friends (true or false) –** A "true" answer could indicate arrogance, while a "false" answer could indicate insecurity. Note: this is a good example of the fact that no one question indicates a particular personality trait – it takes a series of questions and answers.
- **Sometimes people expect too much of me (true or false) –** A "true" answer can indicate a person who can be overwhelmed in stressful situations, while a "false" answer may indicate a person who is too sure of him or herself and won't ask for help when it's needed.
- **Select the statement below that most closely matches your**

viewpoint and the statement that least matches your viewpoint:

a) I don't always need to be in charge of things

b) You have to hurt other people at times in order to get ahead

c) I get mad when people talk about me behind my back

d) If I don't know anyone at a party I'll go up to the first person I see and start a conversation -

The answers given to this type of question can indicate a number of things based not only on your answers but also on which items you choose to agree or disagree with. If you agree most with (a) for example, that indicates that you may be able to work well as just another member of a group. However, if you disagreed most with (a) you probably tend to be controlling and feel a need to be the leader when you're assigned to work in a group.

The Case Against Personality Tests for Job Seekers

Q: Is personality "profiling" a good indicator of which job applicant to hire?

A:One of the primary reasons companies give for using personality tests is that they provide a "profile" of each applicant which can be compared to the personality profiles of successful employees already working for the organization. The problem is that in general it's job skills that matter, not your personality. Here's a case in point (from the author's own experience):

A company I worked for years ago had two salespeople in one of the district offices, call them John and Jack. John was younger, personable and low-key as a salesman. Jack was older and aggressive as a salesman to the point of almost bullying prospective customers. Both were knowledgeable about the product they were selling and neither one made any attempt to mislead a prospect about what the product could do for them – and both were very successful. John tended to close sales by being straightforward and patient with prospects while Jack tended to push for a sale, and almost intimidated prospects into signing an order. If personality testing (or personality "profiling") had been popular back then it's hard to believe that both John and Jack would have been hired. No matter which profile the company had been looking for, a good employee would have been lost.

An additional problem with personality profiling is that hiring new employees based on some "template" of what a successful employee is like can lead to a company of employees who are all very similar in personality. Diversity in your employees (and their personalities) can produce different approaches to achieving the company's goals and can be one of the organization's most valuable resources.

Q: What are some of the other problems with using personality assessments to choose among job applicants?
A: Along with "profiling", problems with personality assessments include:
- Employers tend to look for people who they think are good fits for the position that's being offered and one of the most common

assumptions is that someone who is more extroverted is a better choice for a position that involves a good deal of contact with clients. However, suppose you have two applicants, one whose test score indicates an extroverted personality and one whose score indicates more of an introverted personality. What if the extroverted individual tends to like to "chat" with clients and doesn't always listen carefully and the introverted individual is friendly with clients but doesn't take up a lot of their time and also listens carefully to what the client is saying. Which person will make a better hire?

- Tests with questions that almost answer themselves are another problem. For example, take the question "When I get angry with someone at work who said something rude to me, I: a) stop talking to them and avoid them, b) tell myself I'm over-reacting and let it go, c) confront the person again and demand an apology. Most test takers will choose (b), the "reasonable" answer because they don't want to seem childish or

too aggressive.
- Or there are questions that could be answered in different ways depending on the situation. For example, "I feel stressed when others rush me" - agree strongly, agree somewhat, no opinion, disagree somewhat, disagree strongly. Most of us feel stressed when we're being rushed. How strongly we feel stressed may depend on the importance of what we're doing, who's rushing us and exactly how hard we're being rushed.
- The test taker knows he or she is being evaluated based on their "score" on the test which can skew the results. The applicant may not be trying to "cheat" on the test but that doesn't mean that he or she is answering freely either.
Considering that a job offer may be riding on the outcome, applicants generally are trying hard to pick answers that present themselves in the best possible light.
- Some of the most-used personality tests produce different results if the same person takes the test multiple times. For example, about 50 percent of people who take the

Myers-Briggs assessment quiz get a different result if they take the test again even just a few weeks later.

- Does having similar personality traits really mean two different people will work well together? Probably no more so than believing that a man and woman who have very similar personalities will automatically make a good couple?
- Possibly most important – there's very little to suggest that personality traits have any direct connection to job performance. Personality tests may help indicate a potential employee's areas of strength and weakness, or how he or she would "fit" into a team, but assessments of this type are not a cut-and-tried guide to how a particular individual is going to act (or react) to different situations at work.

"Passing" a Personality Test

Q: Are there any tips for doing well on personality tests?
A: Try to choose answers that indicate positive character traits. That is, answers that project the image of a person who is responsible, conscientious, dependable, imaginative, sociable, tolerant, emotionally stable, goal-oriented and trustworthy. In general, avoid answers that may indicate a disregard for rules, prejudice, a tendency to be overly emotional, a lack of self-confidence, or a problem dealing with stressful situations.

Q: What are some things to watch out for on personality assessments?
A: "Hot button" questions such as those dealing with personal integrity ("is it OK to occasionally take some minor office supply items home for personal use?") or with personal development ("do you tend to follow proven methods for handling problems that arise at work or do you tend to spend time looking for more creative solutions?"). In addition, for questions that offer a range of responses such as "always, often, sometimes, rarely or never", try to stay toward the middle of the range on most questions –

answers at either extreme can be looked at unfavorably. There are exceptions though, such as integrity type questions or questions where a strong answer may be seen as indicating an assured, self-confident personality.

One other thing to be aware of is consistency. Personality tests often include basically the same question repeated in various places in the test. That's designed to catch someone trying to give the "correct" answer rather than what he or she really feels. Whether you're trying to select the answers you think the employer is looking for or not, look for repeat questions and try to keep your answers consistent.

And finally, use common sense – most organizations are looking for people who are confident but not bull-headed, dedicated but well-rounded (not a total workaholic), and able to work with others without causing friction. Just keep those attributes in mind as you go through the assessment.

Q: How do I know what type of answers the employer is looking for (aggressive, middle of the road, humble)?

A: Odds are, you don't know. You can do some research on the employer before you take the assessment to try to get a feel for what type of individual the organization is searching for, but your best bet is usually to answers the questions on the personality assessment as if you were the employer – choose the answers that would impress you.

Q: Are there drawbacks to trying to slant your answers toward what you think the employer wants?
A: The problem with trying to guess the "right" answers is that you end up trying to be someone other than yourself. That may or may not get you in the door, but if you didn't answer the questions honestly you may be trying to fit yourself into a job that just doesn't suit you.

Experimenting with Personality Tests

Note: The author asked a friend (call him Ed) to take one of the free personality assessments available online (one of the assessments based on the "Big Five" model) – once in the evening after a tough day of dealing with clients and again later on a Saturday morning when he was looking forward to the weekend.

Q: Was there a noticeable difference in the results?
A: Yes, even though it was the same test the results were considerably different.

Q: What traits did the test measure?
A: The assessment scores each person on five categories:

1) *Openness to experience* – a low score indicates traits such as "traditionalist", "down-to-earth", "practical", "conservative", while a high score indicates traits such as "imaginative", "open-minded" and "experimental".

2) *Conscientiousness* – a low score indicates traits such as "spontaneous", "disorganized", and

"prefers flexible plans", while a high score indicates traits such as "disciplined", "efficient" and "well-organized".

3) *Extraversion* – a low score indicates traits such as "reserved", "formal", and "serious", while a high score indicates traits such as "outgoing", "friendly", and "enjoys working with others".

4) *Agreeableness* – a low score indicates traits such as "hard-headed", "sceptical", and "competitive", while a high score indicates traits such as "compassionate", "good-natured", and "easy to please".

5) *Natural reactions* – a low score indicates traits such as "relaxed" and "not easily upset", while a high score indicates traits such as "given to feelings of anxiety" and "prone to worry".

Q: What did the results from the first test look like?
A: Here are Ed's scores on the test he took after a long day of working out problems with different clients:

- *Openness to experience: 45 (on a scale of 1 to 100)*
- *Conscientiousness: 33*

34

- *Extraversion: 14*
- *Agreeableness: 45*
- *Natural Reactions: 54*

Q: And the results of the second test?

A: Here are those scores:
- *Openness to experience: 72*
- *Conscientiousness: 24*
- *Extraversion: 86*
- *Agreeableness: 65*
- *Natural Reactions: 18*

Q: What do the two scores indicate?

A: Let's take the results by category:

1) *Openness* – Ed's score for openness to new experiences and willingness to be open-minded went up considerably when he was well-rested and excited about the week-end, so that seems to make sense.

2) *Conscientiousness* – The score for conscientiousness went down on the second test which also seems to make sense. Looking forward to the weekend, Ed would naturally be more relaxed and spontaneous – less concerned with precise planning.

3) *Extraversion* – There was a big jump in Ed's extraversion score on

the second test which could have to do with having had to deal with client problems all day when he took the first test. Usually after a day like that most of us tend to want a little quiet time and aren't as inclined to socialize.

4) *Agreeableness* – Ed's agreeableness score also took a significant jump on the second test. Again, that makes sense – when Ed took the first test he may very well have been less "good-natured" after a long hard day at work.

5) *Natural reactions* – Ed's score in this category dropped considerably on the second test. According to the explanation given on the test site that would indicate that he was more prone to worrying when he took the test on Saturday. Considering how the other scores seemed to make sense, it may be that Ed was simply more focused on staying calm in stressful situations on a work day. Or he may have been a little anxious to get the second test over and done with and get his weekend underway when he took the test on Saturday.

Q: So what does all this mean?
A: It seems to indicate that at least for this personality test the results may be very dependent on the test-taker's situation and frame of mind. Based on the relative scores in the "Natural reactions" category, it may also show that personality trait indicators can be open to more than one interpretation, since you would expect Ed to be more relaxed and less "prone to worry" heading into a weekend. The bottom line? In this particular case, the test came up with scores that seem to accurately reflect Ed's personality – at a particular time.

Popular Tests – the 16 Personality Factor Test

Q: What is the16PF test and who developed it?

A: It's a self-report personality test developed over several decades through empirical research by Raymond B. Cattell, Maurice Tatsuoka and Herbert Eber.

Q: What does the test measure?

A: The 16PF measures 16 primary personality traits as well as a version of the Big Five secondary traits. The 16 primary traits are:

- Warmth (cool, detached vs. warm, outgoing)
- Reasoning (lower mental capacity vs. higher mental capacity)
- Emotional stability (changeable, easily upset vs. calm, mature)
- Dominance (submissive, obedient vs. forceful, aggressive)
- Liveliness (serious, introspective vs. animated, enthusiastic)
- Rule consciousness (self-indulgent, disregards rules vs. conscientious, abides by the rules)
- Social boldness (shy, hesitant vs. bold, adventurous)

- Sensitivity (self-reliant, objective vs. sensitive, sentimental)
- Vigilance (trusting, accepting vs. distrustful, skeptical)
- Abstractedness (practical, conventional vs. impractical, imaginative)
- Privateness (open, unpretentious vs. discrete, worldly)
- Apprehension (self-assured, complacent vs. insecure, apprehensive)
- Openness to change (conservative, traditional vs. free-thinking, flexible)
- Self-reliance (follower, group-oriented vs. self-sufficient, individualistic)
- Perfectionism (undisciplined, impulsive vs. organized, disciplined)
- Tension (relaxed, patient vs. tense, impatient)

Q: How many questions are there on the 16PF?
A: There are 185 questions on the 16PF and the online version takes about 30 minutes to complete.

Q: How can I practice for the 16 factor test?

A: Here are some websites that offer free sample questions and/or tests:

- https://www.16personalities.com/ - You can take the test for free on the 16personalities.com website.
- https://www.psychometrictest.org.uk/16pf-test/

Popular Tests – the DISC Assessment

Q: What does the DISC assessment measure?
A: It is designed to identify four basic personality factors: Dominance (confident, result-oriented), Influence (enthusiastic, likes to collaborate with others), Steadiness (calm, sincere, dependable) and Conscientiousness (independent, result-oriented, hates to make mistakes). According to the assessment the combination of these factors can help predict how the test-taker will react in given situations.

Q: What are the questions like?
A: A sample question might be: "People consider me a good listener" (strongly disagree, disagree, neutral, agree, strongly agree).

Q: How many questions are there on a DISC assessment?
A: The classic DISC assessment consists of 28 questions and takes about 15 minutes to complete.

Q: What is your "style"?
A: Everyone's personality is a

combination of the four major factors the assessment is built on and your particular combination of those factors make up your "style".

Q: Where can I take a sample DISC test?
A: Here are some websites offering DISC practice tests:

- https://discpersonalitytesting.com/free-disc-test/ - Offers a free 12 question assessment as well as a full 28 question version for $29 (which includes an analysis of your style and suggestions on how to adjust your style to communicate more effectively).
- http://www.onlinepersonalitytests.org/disc – Offers a free short 12-question quiz and profile.

Popular Tests – the Caliper Profile

Q: What does the Caliper Profile measure?
A: It measures 25 personality traits that influence job performance.

Q: What is the Caliper test like?
A: The Caliper assessment is a multiple-choice test with 180 questions. The average time to complete the assessment is 2 and a half to 3 hours, although there isn't any set time limit. You do have to mark an answer on every question or the test won't be scored.

Q: Where can I find practice versions of the Caliper Profile?
A: Practice assessments are available at:
* https://www.calipercorp.com/request-free-caliper-profile-report/ - You can order a free practice test and assessment from this website.

Sample Personality Assessments

Q: Where can I find sample personality tests?

A: There are a lot of websites that offer free personality tests that you can use to get familiar with the type of tests employers use. Here are a few examples:

- www.acejobtest.com – offers realistic questions, simulations, analysis and tips. Sample assessments range from free 18 question tests that provide a basic introduction to personality testing up to $19.95 sample assessments with 120 questions covering everything from conscientiousness and integrity to stress tolerance and leadership qualities.
- https://www.jobtestprep.com/personality-test-free – provides free sample questions and a score report. For $39 you can get two personality tests (one that deals with interpersonal skills and one that deals with core performance qualities), personalized feedback, and an analysis of 30 traits that employers look for.

- https://www.123test.com/assessment-personality-test/ - the website includes a free personality test as well as a "work values" test and a "team roles" test. You can also take a "strength and weaknesses" assessment to help you determine what type of job would suit you the best.
- http://www.psychometricinstitute.com.au/Psychometric-Test-Guide/Personality-Test-guide.html – explains personality testing and offers advice on how to perform at your best when taking a personality assessment.

Personality Tests for Kids

- https://www.personalitypage.com/cgi-local/build_pqk.cgi
- http://www.personalityhacker.com/how-to-know-your-kids-personality-type/
- http://www.proprofs.com/quiz-school/story.php?title=your-kids-personality-type

Future Trends in Personality Testing

Q: What does "gamification" have to do with personality tests?
A: The idea of using personality assessments that are in a game format is to make the "testing" more enjoyable and relaxing. Presumably that will lead to employers gaining a more straightforward and accurate picture of the individuals taking the test, with less focus on trying to choose the "right" answer.

Q: What about an example of gamification?
A: Pymetrics.com offers a selection of brain games based on neuroscience that claim to be able to be used to match an individual's abilities to an employer's needs.

Q: How are social media affecting personality testing?
A: New companies are springing up that gather data on job applicants from information the prospect has shared on Facebook, LinkedIn, Twitter and other online sources. Then an algorithm of some type is applied to the collected

data in order to create a personality profile of the applicant.

Q: What is "collective intelligence" and how does it apply to personality testing?
A: Collective intelligence (or crowd-sourcing) is the collection of opinions about a person from his or her past and current co-workers. Those opinions can form a picture of how well the individual may fit a particular job opening and what kind of job performance a prospective employer might expect.

Q: Why are so many companies working on using social media to build a "personality profile" of Internet users like yourself?
A: These "profiles" help the companies to design their marketing campaigns with greater precision – and may even make it possible for them to influence different groups based on their common personality traits.

Q: Have movies shown us future possibilities in personality testing?
A: Well, maybe. If someone can come up with a working example of the "sorting hat" in Harry Potter that measured the temperament of new

students at Hogwarts.

Appendix A – Terminology

Abilities testing – Measuring an individual's capacity to handle a wide range of tasks.

Acquiescence – The tendency to automatically accept a test item as true.

Apophenia – Perceiving patterns or connections in random or meaningless data (a term sometimes applied to personality testing by those who don't believe in the connection between personality traits and job performance).

Aptitude testing – Measuring how well an individual can apply a particular skill to certain tasks.

Behavioral Approach System (BAS) - Brain system that underlies the tendency to seek out pleasant stimuli.

Behavioral Inhibition System (BIS) - Brain system that underlies the tendency to avoid unpleasant stimuli.

Belbin team roles – Dr. Meredith Belbin developed the Belbin concept of team roles in the late 1970s. Belbin's work suggested that a team made up of people with differing personalities is generally more successful than one that's more homogenous.

Emotional Intelligence (EI) – The ability to recognize, control and express your own emotions and to recognize and respond appropriately to other people's emotions.

Empirical Keying Method – A method of personality test construction that assumes that certain types of people have distinctive ways of answering certain questions.

Extraversion - Trait associated with sociability and positive attitude.

Factor Analytic Method – A method of personality test construction that's based on statistics. Researchers administer tests with a long list of objective items to a large number of people and then look for patterns of items that tend to be answered the same way by a significant number of the participants. Once a pattern is determined a "personality factor" is assigned to each of those items.

Four Temperaments – The idea of relating personality to combinations of four different temperaments has been around since at least 600 B.C. There are different forms of these four "humours", but one of the more widely accepted versions is made up of the following moods: cheerful, somber, enthusiastic and calm.

Heritability – The degree to which variation among individuals can be attributed to genetic factors.

Impulsivity – A personality trait characterized by acting on impulse, lack of planning, liveliness, and risk-taking.

Ipsative score – A test result presented in relative rather than absolute terms.

Likert scale – A method used to translate the results of an objective personality test into an assessment of the test-taker's personality.

Objective personality tests – Objective or self-report inventory tests involve the test-taker responding to a series of questions or statements by rating how closely each one corresponds to his or her own behavior. A sample statement might be: "I like to spend the majority of my free time going out with my friends", with possible responses ranging from "strongly agree" to "strongly disagree".

Psychometrics – A field of study dealing with the theories and techniques involved in psychological measurements.

Projective personality test – A test in which the individual offers responses to ambiguous words or images (a Rorschach blot test for example). This type of test is designed to uncover unconscious thoughts and urges – the theory is that by providing a question or image that's unclear the test-taker's responses tend to reveal his or her underlying beliefs and attitudes.

Rational test construction – A method of personality test construction that relies on compiling items that seem to be obviously and directly related to what the test is designed to measure.

Response style – The tendency to mark a question a certain way regardless of the actual content of the question. The phrasing of a question or the desire to come up with the "right" answer can lead a test-taker to produce inaccurate or untruthful answers.

Self-concept - A person's self definition, a consistent set of assumptions that a person has about himself or herself.

Self-report questionnaire – A personality assessment consisting of a list of statements about the test-taker, which the person has to respond to in some way, such as "true" or "false".

Situational Judgment Tests – SJTs are designed to evaluate how you would respond to various hypothetical situations in the workplace. You're presented with a scenario and asked to choose the most effective response from a list of possible choices.

Structured personality tests – Tests that provide a statement, usually of the self-report variety, and require the test-taker to choose between two or more alternative responses

Test evaluation strategies:
  - **Deductive** – Evaluating test responses on the basis of reason and deductive logic.

- **Logical content** – Taking the person's test responses at face value and assuming they reflect that individual's true personality.
- **Theoretical** – Evaluating test responses based on a theory about a particular personality trait – every response is viewed in light of its connection to that personality trait.
- **Empirical (also known as External or Criterion Group)** – Relies on previous data and statistical analysis to determine the meaning of test responses.

Trait (personality trait) – A relatively stable personality characteristic that causes a person to tend to react in a certain way in a given situation.

Trait theory – A theory that a person's basic character traits remain relatively stable after age 20 or so. That is, a loud, boisterous person will tend to remain loud and boisterous and a quiet, introverted person will tend to remain quiet and introverted.

Printed in Great Britain
by Amazon

23372188R00036